Y0-BSN-678

George Frideric
HANDEL

Chandos Anthem No. 9
O Praise the Lord With One Consent
HWV 254

Psalms 117, 135, 148 from
Nahum Tate and Nicolas Brady's
New Version of the Psalms

(Seiffert/Päsler)

Vocal Score
Klavierauszug

SERENISSIMA MUSIC, INC.

CONTENTS

ORCHESTRA

2 Flutes, 2 Oboes, 2 Clarinets, 2 Bassoons

2 Horns, 2 Trumpets, 3 Trombones

Timpani

Violin I, Violin II, Viola, Violoncello, Double Bass

Duration: ca. 32 minutes

Premiere: St. Lawrence's Church, Cannons Park, Edgeware - 1718

Chandos Anthem No. 9

O Praise the Lord With One Consent
(Psalm 135)

1. Chorus

G. F. Handel, HWV 254
Ed. Max Seiffert
Piano Reduction by Karl Päsler

SERENISSIMA MUSIC, INC.

Z5139   *Masters Music Publications, Inc., Sole Agents*

4

6

8

10

12

Z5139

16

Z5139

2. Air

24

3. Air

28

Z5139

4. Air

5. Chorus

Z5139

poco a poco

36

Z5139

38

Z5139

40

Z5139

44

48

Z5139

6. Air

7. Chorus

Z5139

54

58

Z5139

8. Chorus

66

68

Z5139